FACES of AUTISM

Shine bright!
♥ Tere

FACES *of* AUTISM

inspiration. admiration. celebration.

TERA GIRARDIN

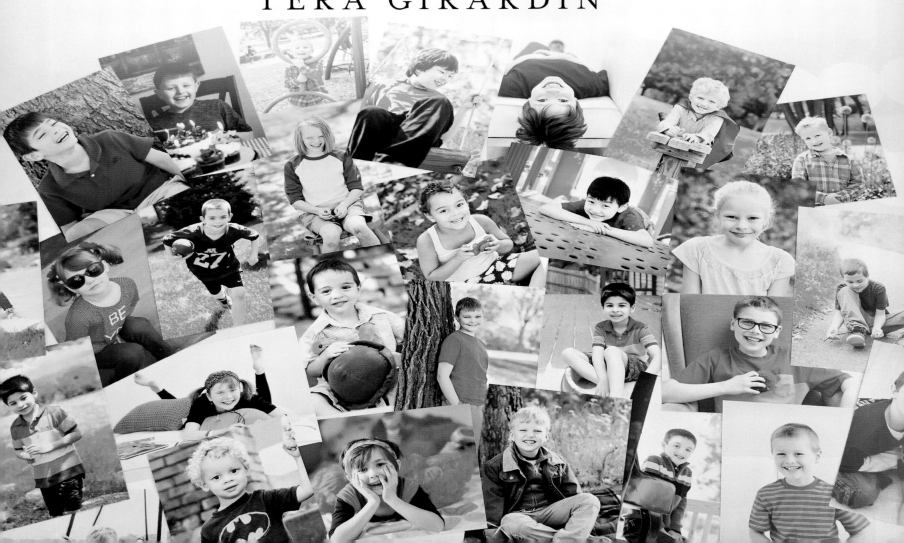

Print ISBN 13: 978-1-63489-055-7

Library of Congress Catalog Number: 2017934010

Printed in the United States of America
First Printing: 2017
21   20   19   18   17   5   4   3   2   1

Photography by Tera Girardin, Tera Photography, LLC.
Cover and interior design by James Monroe Design, LLC.

Wise Ink, Inc.
837 Glenwood Avenue,
Minneapolis, Minnesota 55405

wiseinkpub.com • facesofautismbook.com
Reseller discounts available.

Dedicated to all children with autism.

CONTENTS

Introduction 1

A Special Letter to Children with Autism 5

Landon
Strong 7

Elsie
SPRIGHTLY II

Alex
ENCHANTING I3

Gwen & Griffin
SPARKLY & INFECTIOUS I5

Bennett
BEAMING I7

Jared
BEAUTIFUL I9

Aidan
LUMINOUS 2I

Brayden
ACTIVE 23

Mitchell
RESILIENT 27

Brock
IMAGINATIVE 29

Bryce
WITTY 3I

Josiah
SURPRISING 33

Max
GENTLE 35

Rowan
COMPASSIONATE 37

Spencer
DAUNTLESS 39

Jonathan
PERSISTENT 41

Josephine & Theodore
SENSITIVE & CHARMING 43

Charlie
SWEET 47

Liz
LOVING 49

Noah
SOCIAL 51

Ada
BRAVE 55

Oliver
CURIOUS 57

Truman
JOYFUL 59

Aidan
PLAYFUL 61

Jacob
OBSERVANT 65

April
UNIQUE 67

Liam
ZEALOUS 69

Nolan
TENDER 71

Alex
TENACIOUS 73

FINAL THOUGHTS 75

MY HEARTFELT GRATITUDE 76

ABOUT THE AUTHOR 79

INTRODUCTION

I knew. I knew my youngest son, Alex, "had issues." He was two, and something was off about his emerging language skills. He was vocalizing, but it was mostly a lot of prompted repeating, and he wasn't effectively communicating—not even gesturing for simple wants and needs. He also didn't want much to do with the people around him—not his brothers, not his dad, not even me. And the tantrums! To say they were excessive would be an understatement. I knew something wasn't right. And yet I couldn't face the word that kept flitting through my mind even though I tried desperately to suppress it: *autism*. I couldn't even say the word above a whisper. Because what I knew of autism at the time was scary to me. It was daunting. It was limiting. It was forever. Forever! Alex was only a toddler at the time. Those were dark days, and I struggled to get through a day peacefully. I knew he needed help, yet I was afraid of what that would mean. I felt helpless and hopeless. I didn't want to face that it was autism. I was in denial.

I vividly recall a conversation with his early childhood teacher, who called me at home to gently tell me she thought he should be evaluated for autism. Immediately, my mama bear defensiveness kicked in, and thoughts like,

How dare she?! and *He's not autistic! He's just quirky!* began running through my mind. My heart was racing, and I could feel an angry flush come over me. I quickly ended the conversation before I said something I regretted and stormed into my husband's office, where I collapsed into a hyperventilating, ugly cry because I knew she was right. I wasn't sure I could face what that meant, though.

Once I calmed down and took a breath, I realized Alex was the same little boy with the smile that lit up his whole face. And I loved him with all my heart. So, drawing from a well of patience and determination I didn't know I was capable of, I got to work. I went into research mode, as parents often do when their child needs help. I began concentrated efforts to improve his communication skills at home. I started telling others my concerns, quietly at first as I settled into this new reality. I asked questions. I looked for the best places to get him the help he needed. I fiercely believed there was more for him than the worst-case scenarios running amok in my brain.

At almost four years old, Alex began attending an early intervention therapy center eight hours a day, five days a week, year-round. The first day I dropped him off, I got into my car, and for the first time in what seemed like forever, I felt a tremendous wave of relief from the help-lessness and the hopelessness. Alex immediately began making progress on things that I thought would take years to accomplish. He was doing simple but monumental things, like brushing his teeth, using his imagination when he played with his toys, and calling me "Mom." These things I took for granted with my older two sons.

I spent a lot of time waiting in the lobby at drop off and pick up. I started to notice the other children in the center were making significant progress, too. This was amazing to me! Did anyone else see this? Why didn't I know kids with autism could make this type of progress? I wanted the world to know about these remarkable children.

As a photographer, my favorite subjects are children. I love their innocence, raw emotions, and delightful spirits. I felt compelled to photograph these children with autism in particular and tell their stories. I couldn't stop thinking about it. It was calling to me. Fast forward a few years, and I am thrilled to have brought forth this book.

I've been around and worked with children with autism for almost my entire photography career. I actually began my photography business when I was pregnant with Alex. I didn't know at the time that autism would become a part of our lives and even a part of my professional life. Alex has introduced me to a world I knew nothing about. He's opened my eyes and my heart. As children often do, he's taught me so very much about myself, about love, and about this beautiful, messy thing we call life. As of the writing of this book, Alex is about to enter middle school. His elementary years have been filled with ups and downs, but I'm so proud of him. He has school friends, a great sense of humor, and teachers who love him. He has phased out of needing speech therapy—he can carry on reciprocal conversations and cracks jokes all the time. He has been a student council representative and is an active Boy Scout. In fact, he's spending his first week away from home at camp while I'm writing this. It's nerve racking for me, but I'm grateful he is learning important life skills and becoming independent. And I'm grateful for the lessons autism has taught me: to be present, to celebrate all the little milestones, and to believe more in a person's capabilities than in their disabilities.

With Faces of Autism, I hope to change the way we look at autism. An autism diagnosis can be difficult, but there is beauty and magic in those with autism. As I introduce you to the thirty-one children in this book, I want you to know there is more to them than the difficulties they face.

If you are new to autism, I applaud you for picking up this book. I know you are seeking how to help your loved one. Likely you've done a ton of research already. There are plenty of books to tell you about the ins and outs, difficulties, theories, therapies, facts, data, statistics, and all about how hard autism is. It's exhausting.

This isn't that kind of book.

Don't get me wrong, autism is HARD. It's throw-out-the-parenting-manual-because-it's-in-a-foreign-language hard! This lifelong journey is incredibly challenging not only for the individual with autism, but for their families as well. We need therapies, techniques, theories, facts, and data in order to help those with autism become their best selves. We need to support families and honor the challenges of raising a child with autism. Yes, autism is intense. And it's uncomfortable to those not familiar with this intensity. The easy thing to do is to look away. Or dismiss someone with autism as not having much to contribute. Or worse, to even pity those with autism.

No one benefits from pity. There is no doubt that autism is hard. But in the space of this book, I want to focus on the joyful, light-filled, beautiful souls of these children. I want to change the conversation we have about autism. We've done a great job in recent history to raise awareness of autism. And we are moving toward autism acceptance, which is a step in the right direction. However, acceptance implies tolerance. And who wants to simply be tolerated? No. I want this book to take it to the next level: autism admiration.

What would happen if we were to value autism as a strength? What would happen if we allowed those with autism the space for their development to proceed at its own pace, for their ideas to be considered, for their strengths to flourish, and for their life challenges to be supported? What gifts would they bestow on the world? What if our education systems were elevated to make creative, active, experiential learning the norm? Couldn't this shift benefit all students and be far more inclusive of those with autism?

When people with autism spectrum disorder (ASD) are allowed to foster their creativity and ideas, the world is a better place. Innovators such as Albert Einstein, Wolfgang Amadeus Mozart, Sir Isaac Newton, Charles Darwin, Thomas Jefferson, and Michelangelo all made a significant impact on our world with their life's work. And all are suspected to have been on the autism spectrum.

Who in our midst right now might be the next great artist, poet, inventor, or scientist? Who are we dismissing if we don't value the children today who have an autism diagnosis?

In this book, you might be meeting the next philosopher, environmentalist, comedian, mayor, author, fashion designer, pianist, animation engineer, teacher, sports writer, innovator, or civil rights advocate. The parents of children with autism already know how remarkable their children are, and we want the world to know it, too.

Chances are if you are holding this book, you know someone with autism. Maybe it's your neighbor, friend, or coworker's child who has some form of autism. You want to understand, but you aren't sure how to start that conversation. You want to help, but you aren't sure how. Or perhaps you are one of many support people—teachers, therapists, grandparents, and other family members who make a daily impact on those with autism. You see the struggles, but you also see the light in these children. Or, most likely, you are a parent to a child with autism, and this book spoke to you because you know there is more to your child than his or her diagnosis.

I have the unique vantage point of being a parent to a child with autism, and I am also an observer of autism through the lens of my camera. As a photographer, I am invited into people's lives, quickly developing a rapport to allow them to be their authentic selves in order to create a compelling portrait. I have the privilege of interacting with and getting to know families intimately, if even for a brief amount of time. It's given me a unique perspective. I have experienced and witnessed the deep, unconditional love and the immense pride that go along with being a parent to a child with autism.

Whether you are at the start of your autism journey or a well-seasoned traveler on the autism road, I have a special message if you are a parent of a child with autism.

I see you.

I see the endless things you do for your children. I see the appointments and questions and relentless research you do to get the best possible help for your child. I see the patience and fierce love you have for your children. I see the pain and frustration and tenacity you have. I see your hope and pure joy. I see the quiet way you keep on going even when you are utterly exhausted, because who else will do it? I see the tremendous impact you have on your child. It's a long road, but you are persevering. You are making the biggest difference in your child's life by loving them unconditionally. It's working. I see it.

I see you.

And with a quiet nod of understanding that only a fellow autism parent can make, I say to you . . . *keep up the good work.*

In this book, you'll hear from other autism parents who are eager to share their words of wisdom. Almost every one of them has a similar message: Don't stop believing in your child. Be patient. Life with autism is a marathon, not a sprint (and sometimes more like a slow hike across the Pacific Crest Trail barefoot!). The best thing you can do is to love your child for who they are.

I am so excited to introduce you to the children in this book. You will meet amazing kids through whom you will see autism in a new light. First and foremost, they are children. They laugh, they play, they learn, they love. Some are very verbal, and some are not. Many will strike you as "typical" little boys and girls with their autism challenges lurking below the surface. Some are severely affected and have trouble relating to the world around them. But like everyone, they all have gifts. Autism covers a wide range of abilities and difficulties. And each child with autism has an inner light that shines brightly!

Every time I encounter a child with autism, I am invited to be present and acutely aware of my surroundings. I can't help but see the world not just through my camera lens, but through their lens of wonder and ultra-sensory view. Entering their world takes patience and an open mind, to be sure! When you do, it's so rewarding. During my photo sessions, I've marveled at the sound of the wind with a keenly attuned boy. I've played chase more times than I can count! I've had many magical moments. I've been inspired by insightful words of wisdom from minds too young to know such things. I've marveled at joy and creativity. I've experienced so much affection—from a gentle touch of my arm to a quiet grip on my hand as we walked to giant bear hugs. I've witnessed deep empathy and unbounded love.

The beauty of using photography as the medium for a project like this is that it removes the distractions of autism. Had I used video as the means to tell their stories, you might only pay attention to stilted speech, hand flapping, impulsivity, or slower verbal processing. Perhaps you'd miss out on the inner beauty of the child. With still photography, a moment in time can capture the full underlying beauty and emotion of each child. Photography allows you to see—truly see—the soul within.

As a photographer, my life's purpose is to reveal beauty. Let me show you the inner beauty of these children. Let me show you that *they are magic.*

A SPECIAL LETTER TO CHILDREN WITH AUTISM:

If you are a child or young person with autism, I want you to know you inspire me.

YOU inspire me.

I am in awe of the way your mind works. I am in awe of how you take in the world. I love how present and aware you are and how deeply you feel things. I recognize that it's not always comfortable or easy to have autism. Okay, I'm sure it's just plain hard sometimes. But I admire your perseverance. I know living with autism makes your life challenging—in ways you might not even be aware of, since it's so much a part of you. But I see how hard you work to do things that others take for granted. You are remarkable!

I know your loved ones wish they could do so much more to help you. We are doing our best, but we don't always know how best to help you. But know that you are loved.

You are unique. What makes you unique might be challenging, but it also makes you special. It makes you valued. Don't forget that, because you are needed in this world. Your light needs to shine. Your way of thinking, your ideas, your words, your skills, your super senses, your awareness, your peace, your joy, your love, and your very being are needed. Your autism is your superpower, because without it, you wouldn't be you. And you have much to share with the world.

Tera

STRONG

LANDON

Landon was the first child I photographed for this project. He's nonverbal and can be pretty impulsive, but I wanted to know him beyond his limitations. What brought Landon joy? Because that's what was at the heart of this project: showing children with autism in joyful ways. I learned Landon is a fan of birthdays! He lights up when there is a cake and singing. So that's what we staged, even though it wasn't his birthday. Who cared? He was delighted that we had cake.

Landon's mom gave me some background on his love for birthdays. "For a child who is nonverbal, it's so amazing to listen to him when he hums one of the many, many songs that he hums in perfect pitch. His favorite song is 'Happy Birthday,' so during family get-togethers during holidays, we always try to sing a 'Happy Birthday' song that relates to the day."

Autism is unpredictable at times; in fact, these cake shots almost didn't happen. You see, Landon gets overwhelmed by certain things. . . . In this case, his brother and friends were making a lot of noise, as boys do. But Landon is nonverbal and couldn't voice his annoyance, so his reaction was quick and severe: a sweep of his hands across the table that almost sent the whole cake flying! Whoa.

Landon's mom reacted quickly and understood right away the source of his frustration; it wasn't the cake, but the noise. And after the situation was calmer, we proceeded with the singing—minus the noisy boys and a couple of cupcakes that fell victim to the outburst.

Such is the nature of autism sometimes. I tell you about this part of the shoot because it's an insight as to what daily life can be like. Landon's mom bounced back like nothing happened, because frankly, nothing *did* happen in her world. Autism parents are resilient like that.

Landon's mom is a tireless cheerleader and supporter of her son. I admire her positive attitude so much.

There were incredibly poignant moments during this session, too. I have to share one such special moment for me. After we got the shots of the cake, and everyone else had cleared out of the room, it was just Landon and me at the table. I started to sing "Happy Birthday" again and just get a couple more shots (even when I'm done, I'm never done!). This beautiful child, who hadn't really wanted much to do with me until this point, looked me right in my eyes and using sign language said, "More." He melted my heart! It was the first time anyone had ever requested my singing! That moment of connection was magic.

WORDS OF WISDOM

"Upon getting the diagnosis, remember that your child is the same child you loved and adored before the diagnosis. And realize that although the progress you hope for with your child may not happen at the rate you had hoped . . . there will always be progress. Also, get out there and meet other families that have been touched by autism. You will find the best knowledge, support, and tips from others who 'get it'!"

SPRIGHTLY

ELSIE

Oh, this little girl is such a beautiful soul. Just spending time with her made my day! She's a ray of light, bubbles, sparkles, giggles, and goofy fun. Her mom writes, "Elsie lights up about fairies. I think if she could, she would transform into a fairy . . ." I think she already is one! It's a perfect description for this little spitfire sprite!

Elsie was quite proud to show me her new hammock swing in her room. Her mom told me that sitting in it is Elsie's way of self-soothing; the hammock helps her to calm herself down when emotions get over the top. Having a constructive and effective way to calm herself will help her navigate life's ups and downs. That's a wonderful life skill!

Elsie's mom very eloquently described her beautiful daughter: "From the time she was very little, so many people would say, 'She looks so wise.' And she did. Her eyes communicated so much more than you'd expect from a baby. And while Elsie is sometimes challenged to express herself in words, I know there is so much going on inside of her. Every day with Elsie is a mystery unfolding. It's like living with a perpetual miracle—everything new I learn about Elsie is a gift, and my heart lights up with just the thought of her."

Elsie is best known and loved for the way she greets people. She does so with unreserved enthusiasm, as though each time were a very happy reunion. What a wonderful superpower!

WORDS OF WISDOM

"Always advocate for your child, if ever given the chance. Know you are not alone."

WORDS OF WISDOM

"It is so difficult not to compare your child to his or her 'typical' siblings or peers and mourn the ways they are different, the things they cannot do, the parts of the world they are missing out on. I am guilty of this myself. However, I challenge myself and you to focus on and celebrate the *amazing* ways they are different, the things they *can* do, the world that is so much more *full* because they see it differently and notice things we don't. Take the time to really watch and listen to your child, and marvel at how incredible they are!"

ENCHANTING

ALEX

What's more fun than a boy with a puppy?! Even though they had just met on the day of our session, Alex and Ritter became fast friends—and partners in crime! I'm not sure who enjoyed it more when Ritter "escaped" the leash and went for a dip in a muddy pond—more than once! Alex's giggles and delight when this happened made up for the muddy dog shake after each dip.

Alex's mom said, "Alex surprises us every single day. With his language skills being at the level of a child much younger than he actually is, it is easy to assume he doesn't understand or isn't paying attention, but he *does* and he *is*. Out of the blue, he will say something new that we've never heard before, or make a comment during a conversation we didn't realize he was listening to. He is absorbing *everything*. It just takes him a little longer to process and present it."

I think it's easy to assume a child with autism isn't comprehending or listening when they don't make eye contact. But just because the child isn't looking at you and acting engaged doesn't mean he isn't. Some just process at a slower rate—like a dial-up Internet connection in a high-speed world. Some can't process looking at a face *and* listening to the words, so they avoid eye contact. But that doesn't mean they aren't listening.

"[Alex] is also incredibly attuned to the feelings of others," Alex's mother said. "He knows when others are hurting or frustrated and will try to soothe them with a hug or tell them he's sorry and that it's okay. It has been said that children with autism lack empathy, but Alex shatters that assumption with his genuine desire to make others feel better."

Alex's superpower is how he is almost always happy and full of light—enchanting! "Everyone who gets to know him falls in love with his smile, laugh, antics, and sweet personality."

SPARKLY & INFECTIOUS

GWEN & GRIFFIN

Meet Gwen and Griffin, twins, both with autism. There is energy between twins that runs their parents ragged! Add in autism, and that energy is taken to a whole other level. This pair was busy, busy, but also very happy. Mom describes her duo as "sparkly" and "infectious" respectively, and I can attest to that!

Griffin has a giggle that you can't help but smile along with and a bit of an impish side. After a stint on the swings, we moved to the backyard sandbox. Griffin thought it was hilarious to get his mom to "eat" the dirt by offering up handfuls to her!

Gwen can rock a twirly pettiskirt while shoveling dirt, and all with a fierce look behind styling sunglasses—my kind of girl. I love this image. The slight smile just slays me. This girl is not trying to impress or please anyone but herself. She loves sunglasses, so she wears them. Watching Gwen ride her bike, I could tell it was that freedom and speed she loved! No fear!

What the photos don't show is that both twins are varying degrees of nonverbal. They are both different in the ways they are nonverbal; however, it seems vocal communication is an emerging skill for both, and it won't be long before they won't stop talking. Gwen has a sweet little voice and is very definite with her "No," which is used assertively and definitively. And Griffin, well, he's got his own way of communicating, including grabbing his mom and pulling her in the direction of what he wants—effective, persistent, and all with a grin.

WORDS OF WISDOM

"It's a marathon. . . . Stick with it. . . . Try new things because you never know when that door will open."

Gwen

Griffin

WORDS OF WISDOM

"You are not in this alone! Surround yourself with a positive support system of friends, family, and other autism families who understand. It makes the scary and unknown easier to face."

BEAMING

BENNETT

Bennett has a superpower to brighten your day, every day, with his beaming smile. There was no coaxing or photographer tricks to get him to use that smile in our session! He was so fun and playful. Just like a lot of three-year-olds.

His mom said, "Bennett has an incredible memory and greets everyone he sees by name. He finds happiness in the small things—as one of his teachers put it, 'Everyday is like Christmas with Bennett!' Even with all he struggles with, he has taught me to just be happy in the moment. When I get worried or stressed about how he is doing, he reminds me with a big smile that he is doing great." What a great lesson—to be present in the moment and find joy in that moment.

I asked Bennett's mom to describe something he has overcome or accomplished. "This is a selfish answer, but my proudest and favorite accomplishment of his is the day he said 'Mama' for the *second* first time. It was a word he used often early on but he lost it around thirteen months when he lost all of his language. It was within days of his third birthday, almost two years later, when he said it again. After months of therapy and early intervention services, that one word let me know we were on the right track and he was on his way to great things."

When our child calls us "Mom" or "Dad," it's such a simple thing many parents take for granted; it can even be annoying when it's said repetitively or all day, every day! However, when you don't think you'll ever hear it from your child, it's pretty tough to take. And when you finally do...it's a thousand times more heartwarming than you can ever imagine. I know autism families who have experienced this moment and those that are waiting to hear it for the first time. It's hard to describe in words the magnitude of being called "Mom" or "Dad" or hearing the words "I love you" for the first time. It's one of those seemingly small milestones you celebrate big time!

WORDS OF WISDOM

"Do what you think is best for your child. You will receive a lot of unsolicited advice from people. You know your child; they do not. Also, surround yourself with people who have a child that has similar traits to your child. Knowing people who have 'been there' is key. It's imperative to be able to lean on others for support. Lastly, whether you are with a partner or single, make sure to carve out time to do something fun with your partner and by yourself. Oftentimes, it seems like everything you are doing is related to autism. Your entire world should not be about autism!"

BEAUTIFUL

JARED

Meet Jared. He wasn't really into doing photos with me—way more curious about our surroundings. I don't blame him. We were at a beautiful nature park! Lots to see and explore. But I'll be honest, I was struggling as a photographer to capture his true nature, because I wasn't quite immersed in his world yet, and he wasn't interested in mine. And then . . . he stopped to tie his shoe. And it took my breath away. The light, the surroundings, the pure innocence of this childhood milestone—it was so natural and beautiful all at once. Do you realize the importance of what he did by stopping to tie his shoe? He was self-aware, first of all. He was acting independently and determined to do it himself. And if anyone has taught a child to tie a shoe, you know it's no easy task to teach! But he sat there with a sweet smile on his face as he went about accomplishing his task. No frustration, just determination. And that's what I found beautiful.

His mom described how amazing Jared is: "Many people love working with Jared or having him present in their life. Although he won't initiate interaction much with others, his presence is calming. He's very easygoing and makes you realize that it's okay not to stress out. He doesn't have many worries in his life!"

She went on to describe his superpower: "Many people have said to us over the years that they see light and peace in Jared's eyes." Oh yes, there is an old soul in those eyes! He was very peaceful and calm during our session. It was beautiful!

WORDS OF WISDOM

"It's not your fault. When I first got Aidan's diagnosis, I felt guilty. It's natural to feel guilty, but you did nothing wrong. You have a beautiful child who was given to you because someone up there knew that you would be the best person to raise this child. You are special. You are important, because you have been chosen for this journey. It's a difficult one, an emotional one, a taxing one, and sometimes you'll ask yourself 'Why me?' It's because you are strong enough for it. You can do it."

LUMINOUS

AIDAN

Meet Aidan. This FACE! I love how you can't quite tell what he's thinking; is it mischief? Love? Ideas? Joy? Maybe all of the above. There's a lot going on behind those beautiful eyes! His mom says his sly smile and the twinkle in his eye are his superpowers. They charm everyone around him.

When I asked Aiden's mom to describe him, she wrote, "He lights the way to the meaning of life. I think he was put on this earth to teach us patience, love, and understanding. Before I had Aidan, I didn't understand the bond between a parent and their child . . . and before his diagnosis, I didn't understand him. Throughout the whole autism journey, he's taught me that no matter how hard life is and how many obstacles are in the way, we can choose to be happy, and we can beat whatever's in our way through hard work, determination, and perseverance. And he's also taught me it's okay to take a break when we are overwhelmed. It's okay to stop and take a moment."

I love this photo of Aidan on his bike. Just prior to this, I was photographing him walking around a path in his family's yard. But I wasn't getting great expressions from him. He was doing his own thing, and he was getting agitated that I'd blocked his path in order to take his photo. (Understandable, Aidan! Sorry, my friend!)

So we switched it up. I asked his parents what he loved to do, and I found out that riding his bike was a new-found love. So, Aidan's dad got out his bike and helmet. 'Round and 'round the cul-de-sac Aiden went. It wasn't easy for his little legs, but he was determined. And, much to the chagrin of his dad, Aiden was also determined *not* to wear his helmet. Isn't that so typical?! I love the body language and expression from them both when Aidan finally gets his way and the helmet comes off!

ACTIVE

BRAYDEN

When Brayden's mom sent in their application, I knew her name seemed familiar. But I've been photographing children and families for over eleven years, and sometimes names blend together. I didn't recall who she was until I arrived at their house for a session and saw beautiful images of her children on their walls . . . ones I had taken years before. And suddenly, I recalled that session very vividly.

Years earlier, before Brayden was diagnosed with autism, I had photographed him and his family of four. I recalled seeing similarities between my son Alex and Brayden. Brayden was three years old at the time, and his parents didn't know he had autism yet. I mostly saw the lack of engagement that I usually see with children his age. He didn't really want anything to do with me and my camera. He had a lack of willingness to "perform" and "please" his parents by doing what they asked. He was very content to peacefully watch the clouds and listen to the airplanes overhead.

I suspected Brayden fell somewhere on the autism spectrum. And I could feel the frustrations and worry from his parents that went unspoken. I wanted to say something, but what? Knowing that my own experience with learning my son had autism was a very tough pill to swallow, I knew it wasn't my place to suggest it to them. I saw in Brayden's family my own struggle a few years prior, and I knew they had to find their own way on the autism path. I could only hope for the best and do my best for them that day.

So I photographed Brayden and his family that day with patience and care, loving his unique way of viewing the world, and I went on my way. But I often wondered about that little boy.

And then, years later, there I was on Brayden's doorstep again, and I got to see firsthand how remarkably well he was doing. The synchronicity blew me away.

So what did Brayden's family go through after our first session? His mom writes, "When Brayden was diagnosed with autism at the age of four, I thought my world was crumbling down. I was grieving the loss of a child I thought I was going to have. I knew he was going to face challenges for his entire life.

"Years of therapy turned into years of progress, though, and he has amazed me time and time again. He's been able to exceed goals that I never thought were possible [for him] to accomplish. As a parent, I mistakenly thought I'd be the one to teach my child, but it is Brayden who has actually taught me. We've had many, many plateaus and steps backward, yet he's taught me to never stop believing in him and never stop hoping for progress."

I am so grateful I got to reconnect with Brayden and his family. It really brought home the reason I wanted to write this book: *hope.*

Brayden's mom goes on to say, "When people learn that [Brayden] has autism, I often hear things like, 'But he doesn't look like he has autism.' I have no idea what autism 'looks' like. They'll say, 'But he seems so smart' and 'But he looks at me when I talk to him.' Those things are all true, and I feel very blessed that he is verbal and bright. Most people don't know about all the hard stuff. We have to deal with so much hard stuff, and I would rather just focus on and remember the *awesome* stuff."

Brayden is bright. *Gifted* bright. Math is his superpower—he "sees" equations and answers in his head. (Whoa!) However, that can be overlooked at times; Brayden's processing and verbal skills are a bit slower. Brayden teaches us that we can't judge someone by how quick-tongued they are. If someone takes a bit longer than others to answer, it might be because they are processing things internally.

On the other hand, Brayden's moves with the football are not slow! I had to be quick with my shutter to catch him in action! He loves sports, sports, and more sports. I loved his session because it shows how children with autism are children first. He was eager to show off his moves. Once I was done with the football shots, he wanted to move on to basketball. If I had been willing, I think he would have gone through all the sports with me!

WORDS OF WISDOM

"Allow yourself some time to grieve after the diagnosis. It's normal and it's healthy. This isn't what you planned, but it's your new normal. I can't promise your life will get easier, but you *will* get better at dealing with it.

"Build a network of other autism families around you. The benefits of speaking to other parents who 'get it' are immeasurable. Learn all you can about autism. Educate yourself about therapies, state laws, and what your school district has to offer. You are your child's best advocate!

"Pick your battles. When you feel as though you might lose your mind, remember that you aren't walking this journey alone. Many have walked it before you, and someday you will probably inspire another parent.

"Keep your sense of humor. Autism itself isn't funny, but it sure does create some situations that we can laugh about!

"Don't forget to take care of yourself. Being a caregiver to any child with special needs can be overwhelming, stressful, exhausting, and often thankless. What refuels you? Maybe it's some alone time, exercising, or a hobby. Schedule it on your calendar. Make self-care a priority. You have less of yourself to give your child if you're not filling up your own tank."

WORDS OF WISDOM

"I have so many things I would like to say to help other autism parents, but the one that I can't stress enough is to stay positive. We have had so many hard times over the years, and the one thing that kept us going as a family is finding the positive outlook."

RESILIENT

MITCHELL

Mitchell is a spunky, imaginative kiddo who has not only autism, but also a rare genetic disorder that creates some added difficulties. But that doesn't stop this active boy! We met before his Miracle League baseball game at a wonderful park designed to include children with special needs. He was reluctant to let me take photos and was way more into the playground equipment; instead of forcing a photo, we just played. This actually seemed to have a calming effect on him. He was totally engrossed in enjoying every inch of playground, which made me want to climb on the equipment, swing, and just chill out underneath the cool shade.

His mom said, "[Mitchell's] laugh is definitely his superpower! He has the most memorable laugh that gets noticed by every stranger in the room. When I look at people when he is laughing, I notice the big smile it causes."

"Mitchell has had to overcome many things starting at an early age. He had two incidents that were life threatening. However, the biggest accomplishment of his many

hours of therapy came when he got his eye muscles to work together (this is part of his genetic disorder). When your eyes don't work together, you don't see where things are. He couldn't walk on shiny floors, bridges on playgrounds, or close to any railing. This always upset him when he was younger, and I never knew why until we had him tested by an eye doctor. The difference in his playing, writing, letter and number recognition, and artistic abilities within just a few months of therapy were more than he learned in those areas in the first five years of life!"

No wonder the playground was so intriguing! Time and time again, this was a lesson I learned in photographing children with autism. I could have easily gotten frustrated at Mitchell's lack of cooperation, but every time I let a child be who they are and I step into their world, that's when I'm able to capture the child's true spirit. I think this is applicable to all aspects of life with autism—to meet the child where they are.

WORDS OF WISDOM

"It's okay not to like the diagnosis, and to grieve for what you thought your life as a parent would be like. But also understand that it's just that—a diagnosis. Autism is a part of your child, but it isn't everything your child is. Also, without autism, your child wouldn't be everything he or she is right now."

IMAGINATIVE

BROCK

Since I hadn't met Brock prior to our photo session together, I knew we'd have to take a little time to get to know each other. He had a shy smile and was a little slow to warm up, which isn't unusual. So we chatted a bit first. I could tell he was a little mischievous and just needed some time before his true personality shined through. When I shared this photo of Brock with his mom, she was thrilled, saying it wasn't often they were able to get eye contact from him in a photo.

And boy, did he warm up! I had an inkling that I should bring along my collection of superhero capes to this session. His face lit up when I brought them out and he decided to "fly" at me! It was so fun to see him race around and use his imagination. He'd run right at me and zoom past. It was so delightful to engage with him and witness his imagination! What happens when you encourage a child with autism? They just might "fly!"

His mom said, "Brock is amazing because he never lets anything get him down. If someone is being mean to him, he sends them a big smile and goes on with his day. He always says, 'I just want to make people happy,' and he does everything he can to get a smile out of someone."

Brock's superpowers are making people laugh and telling stories. His mom explained, "Brock can tell stories that are so unbelievable, but the way he tells them has people actually believing him at the end. I always say he would make a good lawyer! He's also able to memorize a full song after hearing it once."

When Brock started kindergarten, he woke up each morning with a bout of anxiety, and his mom would have to hold his hand or carry him to his classroom. About a month before our portrait session, he told his mom, "Sorry, Mom, I don't need your help anymore. I can do it on my own now." Remarkable! What insight and what an achievement.

WITTY

BRYCE

When I pulled up to meet Bryce and his mom, we had gotten our wires crossed on our session time. No big deal for me or for his mom, but I was a bit worried the change in schedule was going to be problematic for Bryce. Most kids on the spectrum don't do well with unexpected changes. But Bryce rolled with it! He was off playing with a friend, but after a quick change into a clean shirt, he was ready for our photo shoot.

I could tell right away that Bryce is sharp, witty, always thinking, high energy, and was probably bored by most adults. I had to keep up if I was going to engage and connect with him. Bryce's mom mentioned that school can be a problem for him because he gets bored and loses focus.

We started with including his new kitten in the photos—Bryce's idea! His beloved "Brownie" was new in his life, and I was thrilled he wanted to share the photo with the kitten. You could feel the love Bryce has for his new kitten; he was so gentle and loving. They were very sweet together.

Once Bryce and I developed a bit of a rapport, we had a ball. He is such an expressive, high energy, and fun-loving guy. Really, look at these faces! I think a misconception of autism is that there is a certain lack of emotion and expressiveness. Not in this case! And that's a good lesson here—no child is alike, and no child with autism is exactly the same, either.

Mom wrote, "I have learned what unconditional love is. Every day is different, and you just have to roll with it the best you can."

I really enjoyed hanging out him. We goofed around a lot, and I could have spent the whole afternoon photographing him. His freckles, laugh, and quick wit had me captivated!

WORDS OF WISDOM

"Never give up, and take one day at a time. There will be good days when your child is progressing nicely, and then, out of the blue, regression will rear its ugly head. So take the small victories and know it was a good day!"

WORDS OF WISDOM

"This journey is truly a marathon, not a sprint. I've learned that we shouldn't judge a book by its cover. We weren't sure just what Josiah was taking in and understanding, but we've learned from him that he knows way more than we could've ever imagined."

SURPRISING

JOSIAH

Josiah is an extraordinary young man who has his own Facebook page already at the ripe old age of nine (with his mom's help). His page, Josiah's Fire, is a growing community with almost 10,000 followers. The things he writes are . . . amazing. Astounding. Wise. Philosophical. Inspiring.

But you would never expect it by meeting Josiah in person. He's nonverbal and doesn't communicate easily. He's fidgety and energetic. He's quick to move and climb. Impulsive. Curious. Full of joy! And he has a big grin. It's hard to know what is going on inside, because Josiah doesn't communicate in a "typical" way. But with extreme patience on the part of his parents, he is bringing his voice to the world. By typing on his tablet, he is writing beautiful poems and inspiring reflections to bring his voice to life. For example, he wrote this insightful piece: "Life will hold some pictures in a dark room for us. It's our joy to look inside it to see old pictures that are new to us when we first see them in a new light." He is the perfect example of how you shouldn't dismiss a person because of their limitations in verbal capabilities.

The journey to overcome the limitations of not being able to speak has been remarkable. His dad said, "The discovery a couple of years ago that he can type on his tablet has opened new worlds for him. We know now what he's thinking, and we had no idea of the depths of what he knows." They tell their son's story in their book *Josiah's Fire: Autism Stole His Words, God Gave Him a Voice.*

"With all the challenges Josiah has faced, he always has such a sweet smile on his face. He is probably the happiest kid you'll ever meet, and his joy is so apparent when he's doing something he loves," writes his dad.

Just like any child, Josiah favors certain toys, and his faves are koosh balls or squishies. You know what I mean—those rubbery, squishy, spiky, funny little balls. And he has quite the collection of them! He brought them all to the studio, and we had a good time playing. They were especially fun to throw at the photographer! Look at that mischievous smile!

WORDS OF WISDOM

"Believe in your instincts about your child. You know what's best for them, even if it doesn't feel like it. You need to be their constant advocate. You may not have chosen to have a child with special needs, but I sometimes believe they have chosen you. Be strong, be loving, and never give up hope in your child's progress. You are the one that will help them be all that they are capable of. And that is an amazing responsibility!"

GENTLE
MAX

"Max is the most amazing child I have ever met. He is the most kindhearted, gentle, loving boy I have ever had the pleasure of meeting—let alone the pleasure of parenting. He asks so little and yet gives so much love to those around him. He may wait for you to enter into his world, but when you do, it is amazing," Max's mom said of her son.

When asked what his superpower is, his mom said, "His true inner happiness!"

I think she's right. When I met Max, I could see what a beautiful soul he is. Calm, happy, gentle, and full of light! Books and swinging clearly bring him joy, and I have to confess, those things light me up, too. I so enjoyed spending time with Max and his mom. There is clearly a ton of love between them. His communication skills are rudimentary, but he was able to gesture and indicate that he wanted his mom in the photo with him. So sweet!

His mom talked about what he's had to overcome. "Max was typically developing until the age of two, when he regressed and lost language and social skills. At that time, he began to quietly enter his world of autism. From that day forward, he has been working so very hard to overcome obstacles that come naturally for other children. With countless hours of therapy, he has learned to talk again and to socialize, and is getting ready to enroll in his public elementary school for the first time."

Many kids with autism love to swing. Okay, scratch that, many *kids* love to swing! (See what I did there?) Often children with autism seek out sensory experiences like swinging, spinning, crashing (like onto beanbags), or being squeezed. For so many of the kiddos I've photographed, when asked what lights them up, the answer is often "swinging." The look on Max's face says it all! It's hard not to smile when you're soaring through the air!

COMPASSIONATE

ROWAN

Rowan is one of those children who is wise beyond her years. It's hard to believe she's just a little girl, until she turns and skips off down the path to explore and hum along without a care in the world. I am in awe of her.

Rowan's mom reported the same: "Rowan is very much her own gal. She goes with her own flow no matter what is popular. She loves the way she dresses. She is a very passionate vegetarian and environmentalist. She is a wonderful artist and singer as well."

I can attest to Rowan being a nature lover, as her first instinct when I was photographing her near a tree was to hug the tree! The love and bliss on her face perfectly summed up who she is.

Rowan is remarkably insightful and well-spoken about autism, too. She understands herself and has learned how to self-regulate. Sometimes it's by pacing in the same circle, muttering to herself as she replays her day and organizes her thoughts. When comparing notes with her mom, I told her my own son does something very similar.

With her understanding of autism, Rowan is very inclusive of all her friends and schoolmates regardless of where they fall on the spectrum. She is an advocate already, and seeks out opportunities to teach others about autism. She is kind, compassionate, and wise.

WORDS OF WISDOM ♥

"Don't be afraid. Do not be ashamed. Kids with autism aren't lacking, they are exceptional!"

Rowan

37

D A U N T L E S S

SPENCER

The first thing that struck me about Spencer is how totally adorable he is! I have a fondness for three-year-olds, and this little charmer was no exception. He was curious and happy and into exploring. I was impressed with the number of signs he used to communicate, knowing he has limited verbal communication skills. For such a little guy, he sure understands a lot. Spencer showed off his counting skills by easily counting to twenty, and would have kept going if I had let him! He clearly understood what I was asking and directing him to do, but having a reciprocal conversation wasn't quite possible yet.

His mom described Spencer by saying, "He's amazing with his beautiful smile and the way he is always seeking out a way to laugh or learn. Every night after the sun sets, he goes to the front window and softly sings and signs 'Twinkle, Twinkle, Little Star' to the night sky." So sweet!

His superpower? "Breaking and entering. A three-year-old should not possess the skill set he has!" A funny comment, and yet a real fear for some parents; many children with autism wander because they are curious and have no sense of danger or boundaries. That puts a parent on constant high alert for their child's safety. Eloping can be a serious issue. But that persistence and problem solving will serve him well one day!

Spencer was a delight to watch as he explored the beautiful spring day. His face lit up as he ran, and I couldn't help but to feel his joy.

WORDS OF WISDOM

"Find the joy and humor within your child. You are a parent first, before all those other things you become as an 'autism parent': teacher, therapist, case manager, nurse, aide, etc. Parent first. I learned to let myself be me first—the other things will come."

P E R S I S T E N T

JONATHAN

There is a special relationship between a boy and his dog, and this case is no exception. Duncan is Jonathan's therapy dog, so their relationship is extra special. When I decided I wanted to photograph them together, I second-guessed myself, as it's not easy to photograph a child with autism whose attention span and ability to follow directions are limited. By adding a dog to the mix (whose attention span and ability to follow directions are also limited!), I figured I was asking for trouble. However, with the help of very patient parents who are adept at kid- (and dog-) wrangling, I was able to capture the special relationship between these two. I asked Jonathan if he would whisper something in Duncan's ear. To this day, I don't know what he said, but I love the dog's expression!

"Jonathan works harder than any child I know, but still shines in what he does. When he loves something, he loves it with his whole being," said Jonathan's mom. She went on to describe what he has overcome and accomplished in his short life: "Every step of development has been an effort. Jonathan has had to work for everything he has done, and yet [he] continues on. He didn't speak until after age four, and meaningful conversations came much later. [Jonathan is seven at the time of this writing.] But today, he can tell you about his wants and likes; he can share his joy and frustrations; and he can be connected with people and peers who are willing to be open to his unique way of being." His superpower is obviously persistence, which I think he gets from his very supportive parents. They never give up on advocating for him to help him to become the best person he can be. And it's working!

WORDS OF WISDOM

"In a world that will tell you how much your child can't, or how lacking your child is, always remember that wherever your child is on their journey, they are perfect where they are. Meet them where they are in their development, join them in their play, and embrace the way they are today. When you accept and honor them as they are, you will see them blossom in ways that the average person cannot even fathom!"

SENSITIVE & CHARMING

JOSEPHINE & THEODORE

It was surprising for me to learn that it's not uncommon for siblings to have autism, which is the case for Josephine and Theodore, two curly headed, beautiful children on the autism spectrum. Their mom said of them, "They have such a sweet relationship. They can make each other double over in giggle fits without using any words at all, and they learn so much from each other."

Both are pretty young, so their autism journey is just beginning, but already they have each overcome some obstacles. "Josephine has recently learned how to tolerate (and even enjoy) water on her face and head. She loves the splash pad now and I'm so proud of her! Theo is learning it's okay to touch different foods, on his terms, and making really great progress."

Aversion to water on the head and tasting unfamiliar foods, as well as other sensory issues, can be a real challenge for parents, as it comes down to basic care for their children. Keeping your child well-fed and clean is at the top of the parenting list, so you can see the challenge. And it goes beyond a "strong-willed" child and beyond any typical toddler manipulation and avoidance. Eating and bathing are truly overwhelming for the sensory system for some people on the spectrum. It can feel like needles to take a shower. Certain smells can induce involuntary gag reflex. Clothing, especially tags and seams, can be extremely uncomfortable.

But Joey and Theo showed no signs of being uncomfortable the day of our session. They were happy, silly, and playful; it was delightful to interact with these sweet siblings. Joey enjoyed pretending to take photos of me while I took photos of her! And Theo shyly clung to mom's hand while remaining curious about who I was and what I was doing. Their light-filled souls rubbed off on me as I left the session, feeling lighter myself.

Their dad describes the duo: "The kids always have a surprise or two for me, but I'm never shocked by what

43

they do. They can always catch me off guard. Joey, with the way she approaches things . . . she can be silly about something one minute, and then step back and really think about it the next. And even though Theodore has limited verbal skills, he has a fantastic memory. It's amazing to listen to him talk about what he learns as he experiences the world."

WORDS OF WISDOM

"Be patient. Our kids are going to do things on their own timelines, and that's okay."

SWEET

CHARLIE

Charlie has the sweetest face ever! But he's not a talker. Autism is preventing him from talking right now. He has an amazing family—two spunky younger twin siblings and parents that are incredibly warm and kind. When his mom and I discussed what makes Charlie light up, she told me he recently began piano lessons. "His musical ability is truly amazing. He has a great ear, and he teaches himself how to play his favorite pieces on the piano. They are usually snippets of classical pieces or cartoon theme songs. He sings and hums tunes all day, and he lights up when we recognize what he is singing and we sing along."

When I learned of this newfound love for the piano, I knew the perfect place to take him. Outside my studio building, there is a community piano. A delightful concept, isn't it?

Sure enough, Charlie *lit up*! I don't imagine he'd played a piano outside before. He tentatively fingered the keys and looked at us like he wasn't sure, but once his mom gave the okay, he tinkered and hummed and smiled an enormous grin! His excitement was palpable as he fidgeted, barely able to contain himself. Can't you imagine him holding concerts in the park one day? I'd love to see that!

Charlie's mom said his superpower is that he is surprisingly easy-going. "Although he sometimes gets upset if we take a different route in the car or if we pass our house on the way home from school to run an errand or pick up food, he adapts and transitions well from one activity to another. He doesn't mind running errands, shopping, or even long car rides."

WORDS OF WISDOM

"Don't give up. Some milestones may take a long time, but keep going. It may not seem like it some days, but we are making a difference."

WORDS OF WISDOM

"Acceptance; when you accept that your child is exactly who he or she is supposed to be, then you will be able to truly see all of his or her wonderful gifts. You will be able to open your heart to give and to receive more love than you could ever imagine."

LOVING

LIZ

Part of the process of photographing the children in this book was asking a few questions of the parents so I would know their child's capabilities. One of those questions was, "Is your child capable of answering questions? It's okay if he or she isn't." I like to know ahead of time what a child is capable of, in order to limit the frustration. I knew Liz wasn't verbal (yet), so I didn't expect much in the way of engagement or communication in typical form. Boy, was I wrong—Liz certainly communicates! Gestures, vocalizations, and budding verbal skills were all a part of our session. The little diva had some particular ideas about her session and how to style it. She had fun moving chairs around and picking out where to sit. And she was very clear that she wanted me in the photo, too, pointing and gesturing for me to change spots with her. It was so sweet.

So we took a couple of "selfies" together, and I laughed at her overwhelming hugs. Such a little lovebug! Liz's super power is to make people feel special and loved without saying a word. I absolutely experienced this first-hand! Her mom said, "Liz is very social. Her smile lights up the room, and she gives the best hugs. If you speak to her once, she will remember you and consider you a friend." Such compassion!

Liz's dad tells of how she is inspiring to him: "Liz has inspired me to be accepting. Every person has such unique struggles and gifts in their lives. She has taught me to be less judgmental of people in this world. Liz has also surprised me with how she is so incredibly happy and nice. It's amazing to me that the happiest and nicest person I know also has significant cognitive delays. She has convinced me that happiness comes from keeping it simple and from keeping close to your family and friends." What important life lessons Liz is teaching all of us!

SOCIAL

NOAH

Noah's mom told me, "He loves to walk trails and around lakes. He loves the outdoors." So a nature park was just the right setting for our session. I've photographed Noah before, and he is the only child I've come across with an extreme aversion to having his photo taken. I've worked with him, along with his mom and a therapist, to desensitize him to the whole photo-taking experience. Now, I don't use the big strobe flashes in general, but I am especially careful with Noah because I know how fearful he is of the flash. Even the click of my shutter would cause him to flinch. We have had several sessions in my studio together, and each time he is less anxious and more comfortable with the process. It's still a challenge, but I respect his sensitivity.

Being outside for this session and letting him get lost in the setting made it easier for me to get that natural, beautiful smile from him. He seemed to forget I was taking photos! He was like any little boy—picking up sticks, exploring the path, and loving nature. It was wonderful to witness.

"You've got a friend in me!" I love this cute pair. Both kids have been diagnosed with autism, and they love hanging out together. When I set up the appointment to photograph Noah, his mom asked if his friend, Ada, could tag along. It was so fun to showcase their friendship.

I think that's another big misconception about people with autism—that they don't want to or can't make friends. Not true! A friendship might be a little different depending on the needs of the person with autism and their capabilities. But friendship for people with autism is more than possible—it's necessary. We all want and need human connection.

WORDS OF WISDOM ♥

"Celebrate the small successes. And get a good team of professionals around you!"

B R A V E

ADA

Ada's friendship with Noah was so sweet to watch. She really was kind and patient and encouraging with him. She held his hand, because she is just loving like that. And she really wanted to include her other "friends" in the photo. "Can we have them in the picture, too?" she asked. How could I say no to this beautiful face? I love the stuffed animals in the photo because they are universal to childhood. The lovey, security blanket, binky, whatever nickname you give it—we all had one.

Ada skipped down the path of the park with her plush friends tucked under her arms as we took photos. Her joy was pouring out of her as she skipped along.

Isn't it remarkable that this sweet, joyful face is also such a brave and determined soul? Her mom used the word "brave" to describe her. I often find children with autism have many layers to their personality, and traits that can seem almost contradictory. Sweet, yet determined. That's a beautiful thing. Ada's mom told me that her superpower is, "No matter how challenging, Ada will not give up! She is my inspiration!"

WORDS OF WISDOM

"Autism may always be a part of who you are, but it doesn't need to define your family. Be who you are, and find a piece of joy in each day you have!"

CURIOUS

OLIVER

This handsome devil is Oliver, or "Ollie," a curious and loving little boy. I loved playing and chatting with him at the park. He reminded me of my son at his age, with his emerging language skills that were still raw at the moment. Oliver was eager to engage and chat with me, but it was a bit of a challenge for him. That didn't stop him! He is incredibly curious about the world and is learning at a rapid pace. When a few bugs caught his attention, we had a deep discussion about them. It was delightful! I know he will continue to hone his verbal skills, and I imagine him giving great speeches one day or being mayor of his city.

For a child with autism, it's not always easy to engage with my camera, or to even engage with me at all. To work with a child, I have to get on their level, sink into their world, and observe what they are interested in. I have to go with the flow and enter their world instead of forcing them to enter mine and making them do things they don't want to do (like smile for the camera). I suspect we'd all be better off with this philosophy. Empathy can go a long way in creating connection.

His mom described Ollie as "infectiously happy and silly." And his superpower is "love." Oh my! I think that's the best superpower there is! The superpower of love certainly questions the myth that children with autism aren't empathetic. And it was clear Ollie loves his mama. She has no shortage of hugs from him!

WORDS OF WISDOM

"Your child is perfect just the way they are."

WORDS OF WISDOM

"Even if you suspect your child may be on the autism spectrum, getting the diagnosis can feel like a crushing blow. Because every case and child is so different, the unknowns are overwhelming, especially at first. And unfortunately, special needs evaluations and interventions focus primarily on deficits—fixing or dealing with delays, deficiencies, even doomsday scenarios. But I see the most progress in my kid when therapists and teachers build upon his strengths."

JOYFUL

TRUMAN

Truman, or "Tru," is one of those kids who just exudes pure, loving joy. His imagination is as big as his smile, and you can't help but join in his fun. I brought out my super-hero capes, and although he didn't share much of his imaginative play out loud, you could clearly tell he was fighting off monsters or bad guys with gusto! His mom said superheroes are right up his alley: "Truman loves anything that pits good against bad or light against dark. He memorizes lines from movies, reenacts favorite scenes, or imagines new adventures with a swirl of lightsabers, masks, and capes. We think it's fascinating and wonderful that a kid who could view himself as powerless has tapped into these other worlds, gaining strength from characters he thinks of as friends and mentors, and sees himself as fully capable of helping the world just like they do."

Isn't that a remarkable way to learn? One of the huge lessons I've learned from children with autism is to see things from a different perspective.

I had to agree with his mom when she described Truman's love for life. "I think there is a widespread misconception that kids on the spectrum are socially detached and emotionally disconnected. But Tru is a kid who craves connections; he delights in loving people up and lighting up a room. He rushes to hug people he knows; he is frequently awed by the cool things around him that most people take for granted. So many people—teachers, neighbors, even strangers at the store—remark to us how much it lifts their spirits to see his giant smile, hear him singing out loud, or watch him jump and clap with glee."

I asked if it was okay to take a photo of us together at the end. With his signature big grin, Truman eagerly sidled up next to me and put his chin on my shoulder as he snuggled up super close. It melted my heart!

PLAYFUL

AIDAN

Meet Aidan. Our photo session pretty much consisted of me chasing him around the playground while he laughed. Little stinker! It was awesome. It was delightful to watch him run and play and create a game of chase with me. Even though getting him to hold still for photos wasn't easy!

Besides the "make-the-photographer-chase-me" game he was also playing the "don't-listen-to-Mom" game. She and I both had a hard time being stern when he was just laughing and laughing. She kept scolding him to drop the rocks (which he was sort of throwing), and he just giggled. It made me laugh, and that was not helping matters, because he kept giggling, and I couldn't help laughing along with him! Playing a reciprocal game isn't always an easy thing for someone with autism. But Aidan was engaged and having a ball! I couldn't quite tell if he was missing the social cue that his mom really did want him to stop throwing rocks or if he was merely testing boundaries as any typical little boy does. Either way, he was a giggle monster.

Sometimes it's hard to tell whether a behavior is caused by autism or whether it's typical child behavior. This can make parenting tough! Other behaviors are more clearly defined. Aidan's mom described how he'd overcome a difficulty with fine motor skills; something as simple as holding a crayon was a challenge, and he didn't want to partake in the childhood rite of passage, coloring. Through dedicated therapists and some really hard work on his part, he has not only overcome his difficulty holding crayons, but actually prefers to trace letters now. "Never did I ever think I would need to ask him to put away his paper and markers!" reported his mom.

Mom described how her son is amazing: "Aidan finds joy in the smallest, most obscure things—a flag blowing in the wind or an airplane landing at the airport. When he sees something he likes, you know it! He doesn't hold back his enthusiasm or joy. And it really is contagious."

I couldn't agree more! His face lit up when he ran. To take time to appreciate these small wonders around us is a valuable lesson that I have personally learned on this autism journey.

WORDS OF WISDOM

"Never underestimate what your child is capable of. Ever. I have been guilty of this. Aidan has shown me that he is on his own timeline and will do things when he's ready."

WORDS OF WISDOM

"Some days are hard. So hard you just want to break down. In fact, it's okay if you do. Autism can be hard and it can be painful, but it can also be beautiful. I have seen my child experience things for the first time that many people take for granted.

"I believe that if you surround yourself and your loved ones with people who care and offer nothing but support, love, and guidance, you will continue to have the strength you and your child need each and every day."

OBSERVANT

JACOB

Of all the children I photographed for this book, Jacob was the one who appeared to have the most remarkable observational skills. He was intrigued by every little sight and sound when we were walking on the paths near his home. It wasn't easy for him to keep his attention on me. Eventually I just started to do what he was doing. Instead of trying to get him to engage with me, I engaged with him. And when I did, I learned to notice everything around me. We noticed the rustling noise the wind was making in the trees, the buzzing of the bugs in the flowers, and the sound of an air conditioner outside the house it was cooling. Just to be present and notice—what a gift!

Jacob is a busy guy, though. His mom said Jacob's superpower is that he is fearless! He is willing to try just about anything. "He loves to test the limits in our home, from jumping on furniture to climbing on the stair railings. He truly is fearless!"

At the time I photographed Jacob, he would be considered nonverbal. However, he can speak some words, he vocalizes, and uses a tablet to communicate. His mom told me of overcoming this communication hurdle: "Just in the last few years, Jacob has become more vocal. He was mainly nonverbal until three years ago or so, when he said 'Ma' and my heart melted. I cried like never before, and I knew this was the beginning of a whole new world for him and our family. In the last couple of years he has gained the words, 'yeah,' 'momma,' 'daddy,' 'hi,' and 'bye.' It has been one of the most rewarding feelings I have ever felt in my life to hear my child's voice."

Jacob is one determined kiddo. "He has the strength and drive to keep going for the things he wants and does not give up until he gets what he wants accomplished."

I can attest to this drive—we took out Jacob's bike for part of his photo session, and he was all smiles! And fast! Again, he was all about enjoying the moment and didn't want to quit when it was time to be done, pretty much like any six-year-old. His mom and I had a workout that day!

UNIQUE

APRIL

In many ways, April is a very typical young teen. She's into the latest music and loves art; she has her own fashion style and a great sense of humor. And she was *not* shy for the camera! Her mom reports it has been hard to fit in, but April is using her diagnosis to make friends and show off her loving side. This is no easy thing for anyone in those tween years! Her superpower is her compassion for others that need help.

During the production of this book, I learned that April made the Honor Roll for her school—something she was very proud of, as she should be! Again, it shows you cannot underestimate your child's capabilities. When we believe in children and their capabilities, they shine.

Sprawled out coloring and drawing, April and I just chatted and laughed. I learned April has quite the sense of humor, and it wasn't long before we were taking cheesy "selfies" together. Her goofy personality and smile lit up the room. That she struggles with anything in life is surprising, because I found her to be so endearing. She walks to the beat of her own drum. I can't wait to see where her life goes—April's life is full of promise!

WORDS OF WISDOM

"Don't sweat the small stuff and enjoy your child's unique spirit."

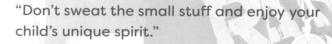

WORDS OF WISDOM

"Be your child's advocate while you teach them to advocate for themselves. Don't be afraid to buck the system when needed. You can make a difference in your child's school, your community, and your government if you try. By doing this, you open up opportunities your child might not have had while leaving the path easier to travel for those behind you."

ZEALOUS

LIAM

When asked about Liam, his mother said, "Liam has an incredible imagination. He loves creating stories, although he isn't always willing to share them with the rest of us. He is determined. It has taken so much effort for him to learn many skills most of us take for granted. But he doesn't give up. He continues trying in his quiet way to conquer his personal challenges. He has the most amazing memory. He is kindhearted and compassionate."

I met Liam at the park where he had brought his soccer ball to show off his mad skills. Like most little boys, he was easily distracted by the fun, and I was having trouble getting a good photo of his bright smile. Add to that some *very* typical nine-year-old boy behavior—being goofy for the camera. I see this so often with boys of his age— they have to ham it up in order to avoid feeling awkward. It was amusing to me that every time I raised the camera to my face, Liam did air guns, or a wink, or the hands-on-hip pose. It was hilarious! And fun. And then . . . enough! I needed a natural look from him, too.

So we bailed on the soccer and went for a walk. Frankly, Liam was a little frustrated—he wanted to do more cheesy stuff, because he was having fun, and I wanted to do less silly stuff. So we chatted and walked and looked at the creek and then it clicked—we started collaborating. I suggested he do some leaps and jumps, and I'd try to catch him in midair with my camera. He was on board with this idea, which allowed me to not only get some silly jumping photos, but also some sweet natural smiles, too. Liam and I went from being a little frustrated with each other to working together on creating some fun photos. I knew he was back on my side when he hugged my arm to see the images on the screen of my camera.

At the end of the session, we had a few more minutes left. Knowing he had excellent self-awareness and some thoughts on autism, I asked him what autism means to him. His insight was beautiful. I'm paraphrasing a bit, but the main part of his message was this, "People who have autism, it may make a bumpy road more bumpy, but it also gives us more creativity. I have it myself, and I think it gives us more of a challenge, but it makes us who we are."

Wow. Thank you for your insight, Liam!

TENDER

NOLAN

Meet little Nolan. And his turtle stuffed animal. Nolan's turtle is very *loved*, and I am pretty sure he loves Nolan back. They are inseparable to the point where it would have been upsetting if we'd removed the turtle for the photos. So I photographed the pair together in our session. Isn't it sweet? I think every parent remembers their child's lovey. The panic when you can't find it. The longing to throw it out! And when they've outgrown it, wishing they would go back and want it again.

His mom said his superpower is his smile: "His smile brightens the room, and his gentleness and attentiveness are a joy to watch."

Nolan reminded me so much of my own son and where I was at with him when he was three years old. Nolan had just been diagnosed a couple of months prior to our session, and his family was on a waitlist to get answers and treatment. Waiting is hard; having a child newly diagnosed is scary and confusing, and it's difficult to see what the future holds. Chatting with Nolan's parents was wonderful; it was like going back in time and telling myself it would be okay. When my son was Nolan's age, he wasn't talking much, either. I wasn't sure what the future would be like. I was so happy to tell Nolan's parents how my son is now entering middle school, is funny as heck, and doesn't stop talking sometimes! It was delightful.

I asked his mom to tell me a little about Nolan, since he was quiet during our session. She said, "He mostly points to things to let us know what he wants and does best when structure and expectations are understood. He's a really smiley little guy and enjoys playing with others. He is showing progress already since he started autism day treatment two months ago."

As no one can predict the autism path each child will take, it felt so good to share a glimmer of hope. I can't wait to see where Nolan and his turtle go!

WORDS OF WISDOM

"Be patient, and make time for as long as your loved one needs to manage his or her challenges."

TENACIOUS

ALEX

Meet my Alex. Yes, my son, and the source point for this book. If he hadn't come into my life to teach me about autism, this book would never have been born. And I'm so honored to be his mom. I am a mom to three boys, and Alex is the youngest. I'm glad I had two before him to pave the way for me as a parent, even though much of what I learned had to be thrown out the window when Alex came along. He has challenged me and taught me extreme patience—I never knew before the depths of patience I've had to muster. And drawing from a deep well of empathy has helped me to understand my son better and help him be his best self, which is what I want for all of my sons.

One of Alex's superpowers is that he has a big heart! He feels so deeply. I think a common belief about those with autism is that they don't have feelings, or that they are cold and don't care. In my experience, it's quite the opposite. Alex cares so deeply that his emotions are overwhelming to him, and as a result, he shuts down. When people are hurt, sad, or angry, he has to leave the area because it bothers him so much. He has been known to leave the theater after a poignant movie, sobbing and wailing because he cared about the characters so much. It's a gift to feel so deeply, even though early on his depth of feeling became overwhelming to him to the point of massive meltdowns. He's learning to handle his emotions so much better than he did during his early years.

Alex likes to say, "Autism is like having a superpower." One of his teachers pulled me aside recently and told me a story. She was having a rough day at school and Alex noticed her mood. He went out of his way to go up to her, give her a big hug, and tell her it was going to be okay. She had tears in her eyes telling me the story. No other student had noticed her mood or consoled her. He does this sort of thing often, and while it sometimes seems out of the blue, he's very aware of how others around him are feeling. If I had to describe Alex with one word, it would be tenacious. He never gives up. Ever. Never-ever-never-ever-ever-ever. Ever. It can be a source of frustration at

Alex

times when he won't let things go, but it also gives him a fierce determination that I know will serve him well in life. In fact, he completed his first five-mile hike with his Boy Scout troop—something he could have easily given up on, but didn't. I understand that tenacity, because it's the way I feel about him—I will never give up on him.

As I mentioned in the intro of this book, as a toddler, Alex's language and communication skills were pretty rough. He was mostly using echolalia (repetition of speech) and basic words, but he wasn't really effectively communicating. He just didn't connect. It was almost like a short circuit from his brain to his mouth. I could see what he wanted to say but he just couldn't get it out. I called them brain hiccups. For example, he could do a spot-on impersonation of *Curious George* with the right inflection. Monkey talk is cute, but not very effective! He was extremely frustrated much of the time. Tantrums were frequent and out of control. But through a lot of hard work at his therapy center and at school, and with the help of countless teachers, therapists, and support staff, he has come so very far.

Today, as a preteen, Alex talks fluidly and without much difference from his peers. He processes things a little slower, but he is funny and charming and insightful. We've talked about how autism is like a different operating system in your brain—much like the difference between a PC and a Mac, or an Android and an iPhone. He thought about it a while and replied back to me, "I think my brain is like our old Chromebook, because it operates a little slower than our other laptops." Yep!

As a fourth and fifth grade student, he was a Student Council representative and had to get up in front of the class to inform them of upcoming events. He is in Boy

Scouts now, earning merit badges and going camping. He interacts with his brothers in a very typical pesky little brother fashion, teasing and joking and bothering them. That's a long ways from his toddler "monkey talk" days!

When he was first diagnosed, I had a hard time seeing his future; now, I know his future is very, very bright!

WORDS OF WISDOM

"Just know that there is hope. There are successes. Your child will grow and evolve, as will you. Not everyone will have the same capabilities, but everyone will grow and change. The little things you are doing that you think aren't making a difference are creating an impact. Don't give up on your child! A parent's belief in a child contains the power of snowflakes, falling softly and gently and, in time, becoming a glacier."

FINAL THOUGHTS

My hope for you is that you come away with a deeper understanding and appreciation for those with autism. Possibly this book has you thinking with newfound respect and admiration for those people in your life who are touched by autism. At the heart of the *Faces of Autism* project is my desire to show that these "faces" are children, first and foremost. Autism just happens to be a part of their lives. But they are children—children who laugh, are joyful, grow, change, and delight in life.

As adults, we often see things through a lens of limitations. It's just what happens as we grow up. The beauty of children is that they have no preconceived limiting beliefs. They just don't! They believe anything is possible. This scenario is so true when it comes to children with autism. We too often focus on the disability and the difficulties. But if we start to operate from a place of belief in capabilities, then autism doesn't have to be a limitation. Yes, accommodations need to be made—new styles of learning and ways of doing things might be necessary to get around the difficulties of autism—but if we change our perspective of autism, then we all benefit. What gifts will be revealed when we shift from simple autism acceptance to autism admiration?

MY HEARTFELT GRATITUDE

The idea for this book came to me as a whisper, a knowing, a calling, an epiphany while driving along in the car (aren't all the best ideas in the car or shower?). I immediately said yes to this muse and agreed in that moment that I would create the *Faces of Autism* book. However, I had no clue how to make it happen! All I knew is that my love for photographing children and my desire to shine a light on children with autism had to be poured into a book. Luckily, I have had just the right people in my life who have been an important part of making this book come alive. I couldn't have done it without any of you!

To all the families in this book who fearlessly stepped forward and volunteered to be a part of this book, thank you. You inspire me! This book has always been as much your book as it is mine. I thank you for trusting me with your stories and for sharing your children with me. They all have a special place in my heart and I cannot wait to see where life takes them!

Amy Quale at Wise Ink Creative Publishing, I thank you for your expertise and for gently guiding me through the world of publishing and book writing. It is through you that I developed my voice and the story I wanted to tell with this book beyond the photos.

Liv Lane, I'm so grateful for your inspiration, spiritual guidance, business coaching, and never-ending enthusiasm. You have been a big part of this book's development (and my development) and I'm forever grateful for your guidance and friendship.

Jay Monroe, your design talent and expertise were meant to be a part of this project. You artfully married my words and images into this beautiful book. And your personal experience with autism has put your heart into this book as much as mine.

Luke Warkenthien of Working King Media, I thank you for bringing my book to life in video. The care you take in your work and your patience with your subjects (*ahem*—me!) shows in every video you create.

Patrick North of Flex Creative, thank you for being such a great sounding board and enthusiastic supporter, and for getting the *Faces of Autism* website up and running smoothly. I always value your advice and expert design eye. I'm grateful for your input on this book.

MY HEARTFELT GRATITUDE

My Innovative Networking colleagues: Meeting with all of you weekly has kept me accountable and buoyed me when my own enthusiasm waned. Thank you all for your support, connections, ideas, encouragement, and friendship.

My "soul sisters," Christy Moe Marek, Sarah Rudell Beach, Michael Nelson, Liz Coenen, Lori Portka, and all my many Infinite Purpose friends: I thank you all for your unwavering belief, cheerleading, suggestions, advice, and your sparkly magic. You have been witness to the birth of this book and I thank you for sistering me along the way.

My actual sisters, Erika Esterby and Andrea Abbas, and my brother Josh Girardin (and their awesome spouses): Thank you for always being there for me and stepping up and doing whatever needs to be done. Because that's what family does. And beyond the book, thank you for being my support system throughout our autism journey. Never once have you been anything less than accepting. You embody autism admiration at its best.

My parents, Joel and Coleen Girardin, I thank you for teaching me early on in life that I could be and do anything I set my mind to. It's a powerful and important belief to instill in a child and I'm doing my best to do that with my own children. And now I'm taking it beyond our own family with this book. My belief in capabilities, especially those who are differently abled, is rooted in how you raised me. Thank you for that and so much more. Oh, and thank you, Mom, for sharing every single Facebook post I've ever posted. You are my biggest fan! (And the feeling is mutual).

And lastly, my boys, Drew, Aaron, and Alex: The three of you have taught me far more than I'll ever teach you and for that I am deeply grateful. I am so proud of the young men you are becoming. I am honored to be your mom. And I love you more.

ABOUT THE AUTHOR

Tera Girardin has been a child and family photographer since 2005. She creates fresh, authentic portraits using natural light. She is eternally optimistic and carries that through her work. Tera is an advocate and a voice for children with autism. Her other writings can be found on *The Mighty* (themighty.com). She is proud mom to three boys. She enjoys spending time at the many lakes Minnesota has to offer, is awed by the night sky, savors quiet Sundays, dwells in gratitude, and is honored to be able to reveal the inner beauty of those whom she photographs. Learn more at teraphotograpy.com.